SCHOOL IN THE USA

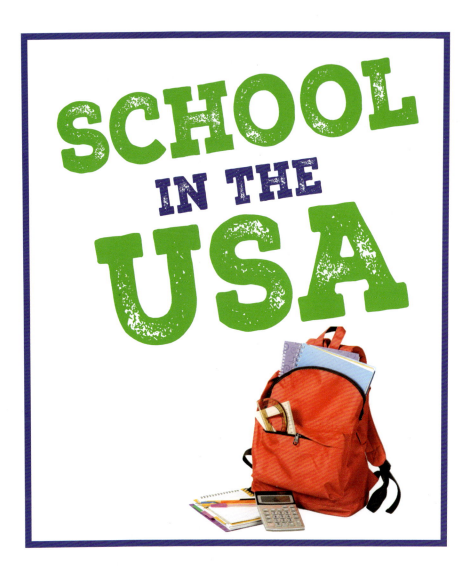

Going to School

walking

by bus

by bike

announcements

agenda

Pledge of Allegiance

social studies

physical education (PE)

elective

Supplies

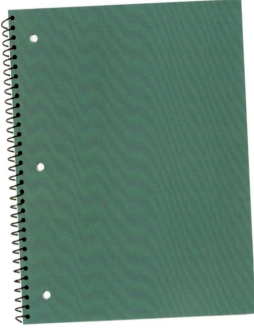

notebook

paper

pens

student ID

LINCOLN MIDDLE SCHOOL

Firstname Lastname   Grade 7

pencil

backpack

Books and Reading

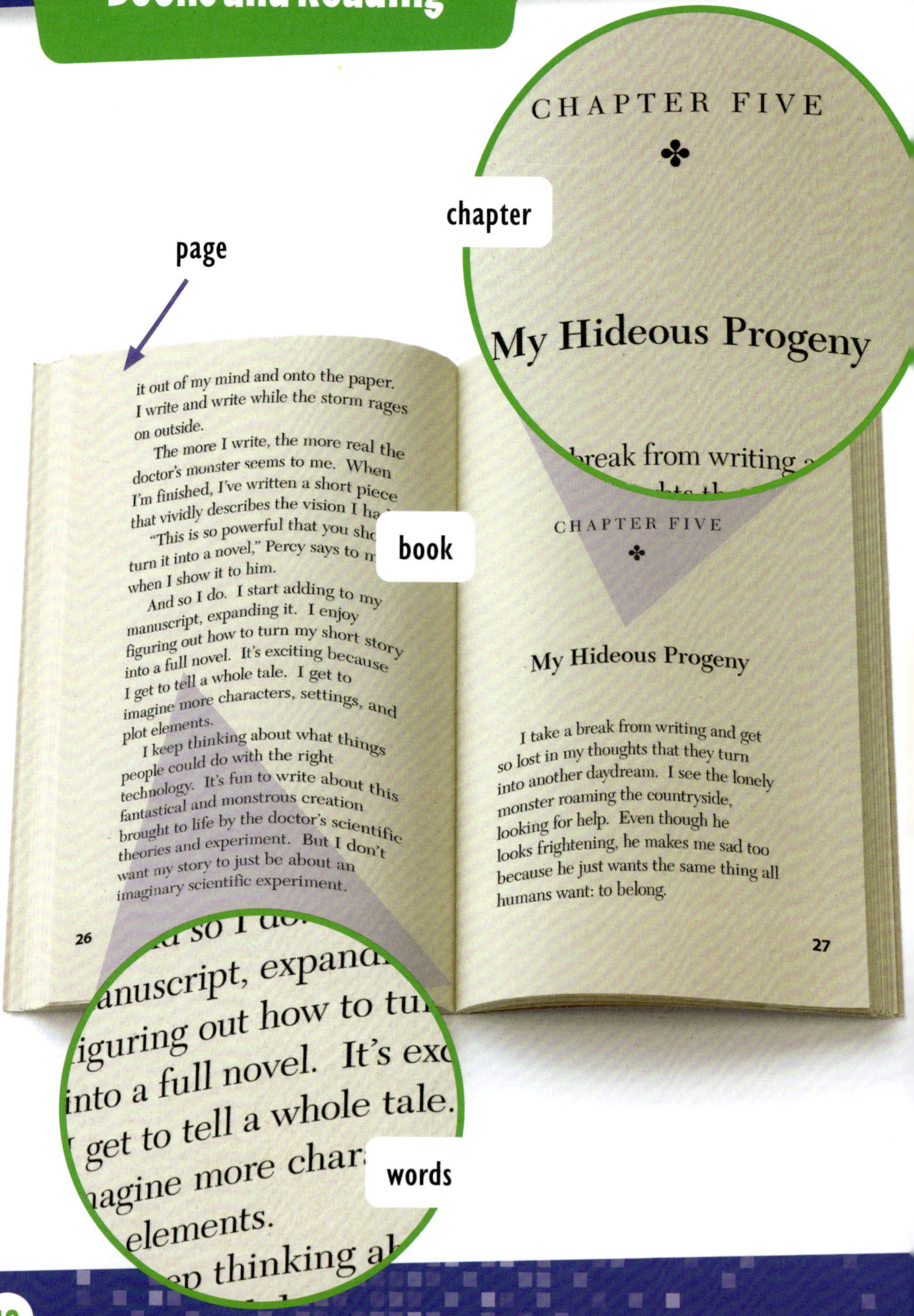

chapter
page
book
words

reading

paragraph

diagram

Changing Classes

hallway

lockers

restrooms

snack

tardy

walk, don't run

Ways to Learn

independent

technology

small group

trash

People to Know

teacher

student

principal

Places to Know

classroom

office

auditorium

Equipment

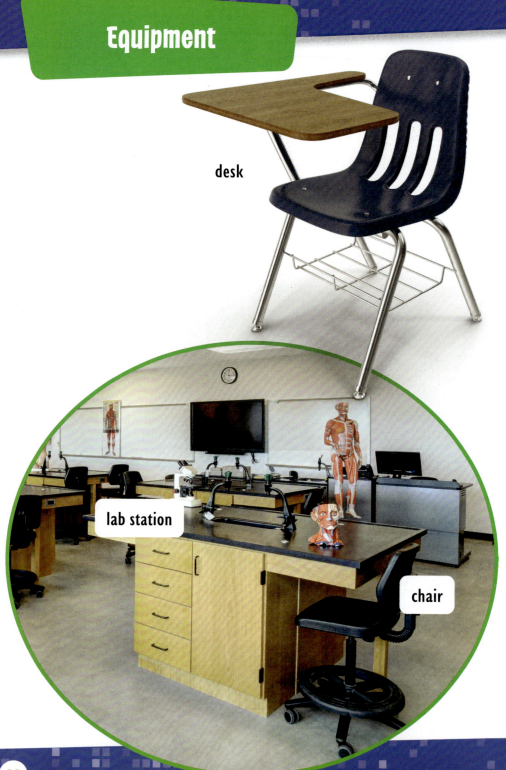

desk

lab station

chair

board

bulletin board

computers

School Events

fire drill

rally

dance

assembly

game

performance

End of School Day

clean up

say goodbye

pack your bag

After School

sports

clubs

Helping at Home

pets

siblings

family

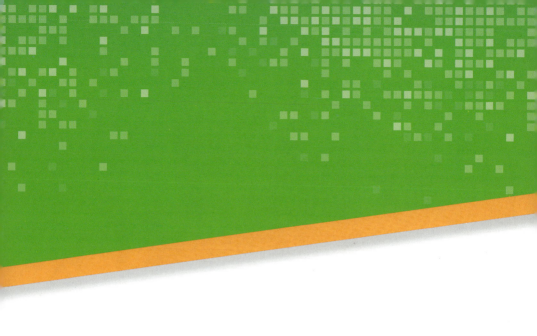

Consultants
Janessa Lang, M.A. Ed.
Elementary Teacher, Los Angeles

Publishing Credits
Rachelle Cracchiolo, M.S.Ed., Publisher
Emily R. Smith, M.A.Ed., *SVP of Content Development*
Véronique Bos, *VP of Creative*
Kevin Pham, *Senior Graphic Designer*

Image Credits: p.5 Marmaduke St. John / Alamy Stock Photo; p.15 Marmaduke St. John / Alamy Stock Photo; p.20 Will & Deni McIntyre / Getty Images; p.20 William Graham / Alamy Stock Photo; p.23 Fred Fuhrmeister / Alamy Stock Photo; p.23 Chuck Franklin / Alamy Stock Photo; p.24 mohd kamarul hafiz / Shutterstock; p.24 Emily Stein / Getty Images; p.24 Spencer Grant / Alamy Stock Photo; p.25 Bob Daemmrich / Alamy Stock Photo; all images from iStock, Shutterstock, or in the public domain

Library of Congress Control Number available upon request.

This book may not be reproduced or distributed in any way without prior written consent from the publisher.

5482 Argosy Avenue
Huntington Beach, CA 92649
www.tcmpub.com
ISBN 979-8-3309-0484-6
© 2025 Teacher Created Materials, Inc.
Printed by: 51497
Printed in: China